The Craft of the
Blacksmith
Llawr-y-glyn Smithy

Shoeing scene, Tŷ Nant, Clwyd.

The Craft of the Blacksmith

Llawr-y-glyn Smithy

JOHN WILLIAMS-DAVIES

UNIVERSITY OF WALES PRESS
NATIONAL MUSEUM OF WALES

CARDIFF
1991

First published 1991

British Library Cataloguing in Publication Data

Williams-Davies, John
  The craft of the blacksmith: Llawr-y-glyn Smithy.
  I. Title
  682.09429

ISBN 0-7083-1108-3

Front cover:
*David Rees Edwards, blacksmith at the Welsh Folk Museum, working at
the anvil in Llawr-y-glyn Smithy.*
Back cover:
Llawr-y-glyn Smithy at the Welsh Folk Museum, St Fagans.

Cover design by Pica, Cardiff

Typeset in 10pt Baskerville by Afal, Cardiff
Printed in Wales by Qualitex Printing Limited

Introduction

The blacksmith has traditionally been regarded as the most important craftsman in the rural community. Indeed, it is difficult for us today to realize just how central a figure he was in a society which relied almost entirely upon the horse for its motive power. In addition it was he who provided the farmer with the implements of cultivation, the housewife with many of her domestic utensils and the other village craftsmen with the bulk of their tools and equipment.

Iron-making appears to have been introduced into Britain around 450 BC and had certainly reached Wales by the third century BC. When the Romans arrived in Britain they found a thriving, if widely scattered, iron industry. The Forest of Dean, on the Welsh border, was one of the most important iron-making centres in Britain throughout the Roman period and remained so for many centuries. Wales itself, however, appears to have stayed outside the mainstream of iron-working during this early period. The Saxons, and the Normans in turn, were very skilled smiths, but the Welsh princes appear to have kept their alien influence at bay. Many fine artefacts dating from the 'golden age' of English ironwork in the thirteenth century are to be found in various churches along the Welsh border, but none is to be found in Wales itself.

Welsh ironwork in this early period appears to have remained purely functional. The best surviving example of thirteenth-century Welsh ironwork, the Clynnog Chest, displays sturdy competent craftsmanship, but with little attempt at ornamentation. Despite the functional nature of Welsh ironworking, however, it is clear that the Welsh blacksmith enjoyed the same exalted status as did his counterpart elsewhere. According to the tenth-century Laws of Hywel Dda, prince of Dyfed, the blacksmith was one of the eleven royal servants accorded a place at court. Moreover, *Y Llyvyr Ddu or Weun* (The Black Book of Chirk), *circa* 1200, states that in the medieval Welsh court a chair was reserved for the blacksmith, as the chief representative of

Illustration of a medieval Welsh blacksmith from the thirteenth-century Peniarth manuscript. (National Library of Wales).

the material world, alongside the priest or scholar who was the keeper of the written word and the poet, as the keeper of the spoken word. It was recognized, therefore, that the smith was the most important craftsman, a status he retained for many centuries.

The fourteenth century was a period of transformation for smithcraft in terms of both

1

organization and technique. To many purists, who viewed the essence of the smith's skill as working exclusively with hot iron and a hammer, it was a period of decline. The advent of improved tools and equipment enabled the smith to work increasingly in cold metal thereby dispensing with many of the traditional techniques. More positively, the century also saw the formalization of the craft in England with the incorporation of the Worshipful Company of Blacksmiths in 1325 and the formation of the Guild of Farriers in 1356. Paradoxically, the same century also saw the gradual fragmentation of the craft in its old form, especially in the towns. Specialist skills, such as locksmithing, the making of armour, gunsmithing and later, clock-making, which had all formerly been branches of general smithcraft, became established as distinct and separate crafts.

In the rural areas, however, the blacksmith remained a general ironworker satisfying a local demand for everyday objects. It is to this rural tradition of ironworking that the Llawr-y-glyn smithy belongs. The Montgomeryshire smithy, now re-erected at the Welsh Folk Museum, St Fagans, is typical of the many hundreds of similar establishments which existed throughout Wales until comparatively recently. Taking Llawr-y-glyn as its focus, this booklet presents an introduction to the work of the rural blacksmith.

The Blacksmith's Craft

RAW MATERIALS

The blacksmith's traditional raw material was wrought iron, a relatively pure form of smelted iron (at least 99 per cent pure), which had the impurities driven out by hammering. Indeed, up to the fourteenth century, much of this final hammering work had to be done by the blacksmith himself. Unsurprisingly therefore, early ironwork is characterized by a lack of straightness and right angles. Wrought iron was in many ways ideal for fine decorative ironwork. It is fibrous in structure and when hot can easily be drawn out, and can be hammered into virtually any shape. From the middle of the nineteenth century onwards, however, wrought iron was increasingly replaced by mild steel, an alloy of pure iron and carbon. Mild steel had several advantages over wrought iron. It was much stronger, it could be hardened to a far greater degree and it could

be tempered to retain its cutting edge. On the other hand, it was not without its drawbacks. It had a far narrower working temperature range than wrought iron and would burn more easily, moreover it could not be worked as finely. Its over-riding advantage, however, was that following the introduction of the Bessemer process in 1856 it became far easier and cheaper to produce than wrought iron. As a consequence, the production of wrought iron declined from a peak of some three million tons in 1870, to one million tons in 1900 and just over 113,000 tons in 1930. Wrought iron production ceased entirely in Britain during the mid-seventies and virtually all modern blacksmithing is done with mild steel. The term 'wrought ironwork' is still used, but now refers to a method of working using fire and hammer rather than to the actual material.

THE FIRE

The basis of the blacksmith's skill lies in the understanding and control of fire. Judging the heat of the fire by eye and knowing the amount of heat needed for a specific task was fundamental to all smith work. Nowadays bituminous, sulphur-free coal is used as fuel, although charcoal was formerly used. The smith has three main aims in managing the fire. Firstly, the fire should be kept small. Any fire which is larger than that required to heat the metal being worked is wasteful. Secondly, the fire must be prevented from burning hollow. Heat is needed immediately below the iron being heated and this is not possible with a hollow fire. Finally, care has to be taken to avoid clinker, a black treacly substance formed from impurities in the coal. In its molten state clinker clings to hot metal making it difficult to work. When cold, clinker forms a black glass-like substance. Constant vigilance is required and clinker has to be removed as soon as it appears.

The fire is controlled by the bellows and fire tools. A blast pipe or *tuyère* from the bellows opens directly into the hearth, and one blast from it is enough to increase the heat of the fire instantly. Traditional bellows could be operated one handed by means of a long wooden handle, freeing the other hand to manipulate the iron in the fire. Nowadays, bellows have been

Blacksmith and his assistant, the striker, at work, Cwmbelan, Powys.

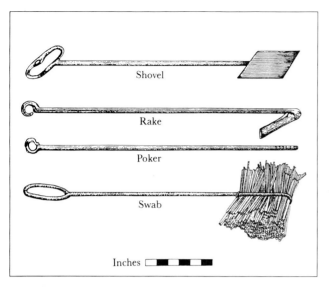

Fire tools.

replaced by electric blowers. A full set of fire tools consists of a *poker*, a *shovel* or slice, a *rake* to hook out clinker, and a *swab,* (a poker-like implement tipped with wet rags or straw), to dampen down the edges of the fire. Few blacksmiths use all four tools and most appear to have managed using only the poker and shovel.

Gauging the heat of iron by eye requires great experience. It is best done in ordinary daylight and for this reason most smithies have both hearth and anvil placed out of direct sunlight. Several specific 'heats' of iron are recognized by blacksmiths, and these are defined in a modern smithing manual as follows:

Warm heat. Metal just too hot to touch by hand. Used for setting up springs without removing the temper from the iron.

Black heat. No colour visible in daylight, but metal gives a faint red glow in the dark. Not used in smithing operations, but will produce a matt black finish on ornamental ironwork.

Dull red or blood red heat. Used to produce easy bends on mild steel and for forging carbon steel.

Bright red heat. Used for simple forging operations on mild steel, light punching and hot chiselling.

Bright yellow or near welding heat. The principal working temperature for mild steel and wrought iron.

Light welding, sweating or slippery heat. Used for welding mild steel if there is a danger of its burning at a higher temperature, but the operation demands considerable skill. Wrought iron can be forged at this heat.

Full welding heat. A few white sparks appear amongst the red ones from the fire. It is the welding heat for most types of mild steel.

White or snowball heat. The correct heat for welding wrought iron, but too hot for mild steel.

TECHNIQUES

There are a number of basic blacksmithing skills which used in combination can produce most desired results. The main ones are:

Drawing out or fullering. Increasing the length of a piece of metal whilst at the same time reducing its cross-section, e.g. forming the point of a bar.

Upsetting. Shortening and thickening a bar of iron in a particular place.

David Rees Edwards, blacksmith at the Welsh Folk Museum, tending the fire.

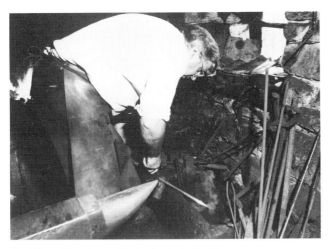

David Rees Edwards quenching hot iron in the 'bosh'.

Bending. A self-explanatory operation, often not as simple as it sounds. Because metal is subject to great stress on a bend it is frequently necessary to upset the metal at this point before bending.

Hot cutting. Cutting hot metal using a special hot chisel.

Punching and drifting. Punches are used to make the initial hole in hot metal. These holes are then shaped and finished using drifts.

Welding. Joining together two pieces of hot metal by hammering. One of the most difficult of blacksmithing operations.

In addition to the above mechanical operations it is often necessary for a smith to change the nature of metal for various purposes using heat treatment. The main operations are:

Hardening. Steel can be hardened by heating it slowly to between black and dull red heat and quenching (cooling) it rapidly in water, oil or brine depending upon the hardness required.

Tempering. Steel that has been hardened is very brittle and must be tempered before it can be sharpened to a cutting edge. This is done by heating the iron to a low temperature and cooling it gently in the quenching trough.

Annealing. A softening process. Steel is heated and allowed to cool in the dying fire, hot ashes or lime.

Normalizing. A similar process of annealing except that the metal is allowed to cool naturally in the air.

Case hardening. A process whereby a hard skin is obtained on steel which does not contain enough carbon to harden in the normal way. The item to be hardened is first placed in a vessel containing a hardening agent. This is heated to red hot and cooled slowly, causing the compound to penetrate the metal, allowing it to be hardened in the normal way.

THE BLACKSMITH'S TOOLS

Despite the overwhelming impression given by most smithies of being full to overflowing, cluttered with tools and equipment, in reality the craft requires very few basic tools. All the tools, however, can be made in an infinite variety of sizes. It was traditional for the blacksmith to make his own tools, starting with the basic types and adding to them when the occasion demanded. As a result, blacksmiths accumulated a very large collection over the years. The basic tools are:

The Anvil. Most of the blacksmith's work is done on the anvil. Anvils were originally made from wrought iron, but modern ones are made of mild steel with a hardened working surface. The London pattern anvil is the one most commonly used. The work is done on the face of the anvil, except the cutting which is finished on the table. This has a softer surface which does not damage the cutting edge of the chisel. The bick (beak) of the anvil is used for bending and shaping metal and is especially useful for the making of horseshoes. The square hole at the back of the anvil is used to hold the shank of various bottom tools, and the round hole is used for punching. The anvil is set on a block of wood, usually elm, which raises it to a convenient working height and provides it with the spring and rebound essential for efficient working. Using a poorly set up anvil has been likened to jumping in sand whilst working on a good one is said to be like jumping on a springboard.

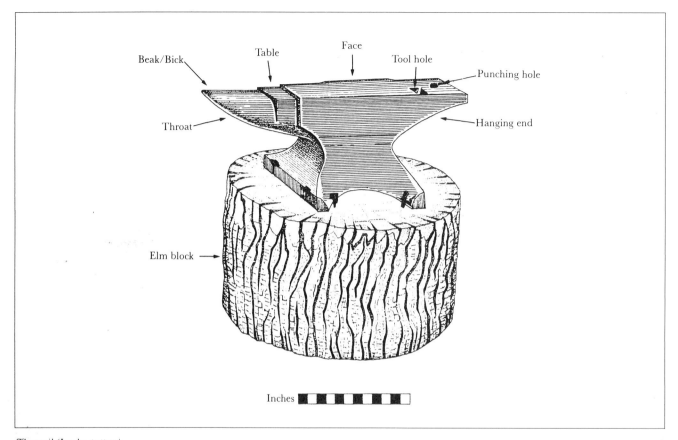

The anvil (London pattern).

It is also important to position the anvil at the correct angle and distance from the hearth to reduce wasted effort. A cooling trough or 'bosh' is used in conjunction with each anvil. Normally this contains water, although oil or brine can be used for specific purposes.

Hammers. Smiths employ a variety of different hammers. The general, all-purpose tool of the rural blacksmith was the ball-pane hammer which could vary in weight from 1¾lb. to 3lb., depending upon personal preference. The length and shape of the haft was similarly a matter of individual choice. A sledge-hammer was used for heavy work and this normally involved two people working together, striking the metal alternately. The blacksmith used a small hammer to indicate where the metal should be struck and his assistant, the striker, wielded the sledge.

Tongs. Used to handle hot iron. Tongs came in a variety of types and sizes to suit different purposes. The handles were usually at least twenty inches to keep the iron well away from the hand.

Mandrel. A hollow, cast-iron cone which could vary in size from one to four feet. Used for bending, rounding and trueing up small hoops.

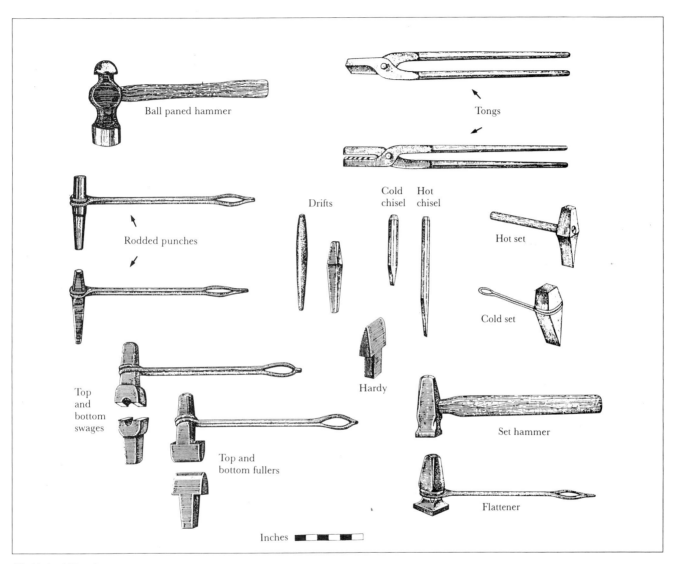

Ball paned hammer

Tongs

Drifts

Cold chisel

Hot chisel

Hot set

Cold set

Rodded punches

Top and bottom swages

Top and bottom fullers

Hardy

Set hammer

Flattener

Inches

The blacksmith's tools.

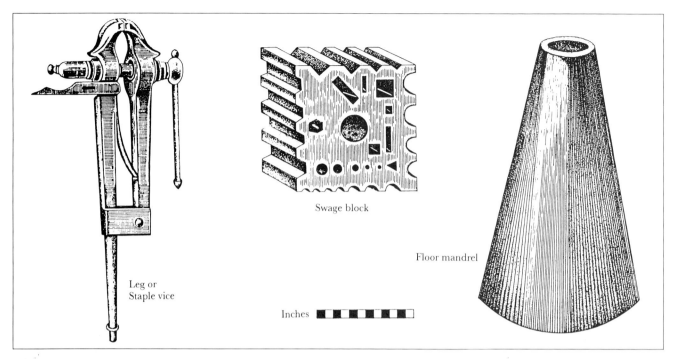

Leg or
Staple vice

Swage block

Floor mandrel

Inches

The blacksmith's tools.

Swage block. A heavy cast-iron block with different sized V and half round holes used to shape heated metal. The swage was often placed on a metal stand and is virtually an auxiliary, specialist anvil.

Vices. Every smithy had at least two types of vice. The large leg or staple vice, often floor mounted was used for heavy bending and hammering work. A smaller, bench-mounted engineers' vice was used for light work.

Punches. Pointed metal rods of various shapes and thicknesses used for making holes in hot metal. They had to be long enough to be used without the hand being too close to the hot metal.

Drifts. Used for enlarging and shaping holes made with a punch.

Drills. Up to the early nineteenth century, smithies were equipped with heavy, weighted beam drills which had a brace fitted below the beam. The weight of the tool enables the bit to drill iron even when hand turned.

These were later replaced by more efficient, metal column drills.

Cold chisels. Short, thick tools of hard steel used for cutting cold metal.

Hot chisels. These were both longer and thinner than cold chisels. Length was necessary to keep the hand away from the hot metal and the thinness enabled the chisel to cut through the metal easily.

Sets. Handled chisels used in conjunction with a sledge-hammer. Cold sets were shorter and thicker than cold chisels and had twisted wire or hazel handles to absorb the shock of the sledge-hammer blow. Hot sets were finer and used for more precise work. Because the hot metal absorbed most of the shock, hot sets could have solid wooden hafts.

Fullers. Round-nosed tools similar to chisels. They were used for making shoulders in metal before drawing down pins and tenons. They came in three types, **small**

Cutting hot iron using a hardy.

Swages. Pairs of top and bottom tools between which iron could be shaped. The bottom swage, fitted on to the anvil, holds the iron and the long-handled top swage is placed on top of it and struck with a sledge-hammer.

Measuring tools. The blacksmith's basic measuring tool was the ruler, usually made of brass so that it would not rust or discolour in the heat. In addition he also used a variety of callipers, dividers and travellers (wheeled devices used for measuring the circumference of circular objects).

fullers, which were hand held; hafted **large fullers,** and **bottom fullers** which fitted into the tool hole of the anvil.

Hardies. Shanked chisels made to fit onto the anvil. The metal to be cut was driven on to them.

Set hammers and flatters. Long hafted hammer-like tools with flat or convex faces used to shape metal. They are placed on the work and struck with a sledge-hammer.

The Country Blacksmith

The blacksmith was a key figure in the rural economy. In the days before industrialization he was responsible for making and repairing the vast range of farm and domestic equipment needed by the community. He produced an extensive array of goods, ranging from simple items like nails and staples to complex pieces of work such as ploughs and harrows and including edge tools, fittings for carts and wagons, domestic utensils and the thousand and one other iron objects large and small used by the local community. The account book of Ben Evans, a blacksmith of Aberbanc, Dyfed, for example, provides an indication of the type of work undertaken by a rural smith. Among the entries for the period 1889–92 are the following:

Mend ploughshare and coulter (1/2)	*Casting [i.e. mould-board] for drill plough (7/6)*
Tip clog (1d.)	*New share (5/6)*
New matock (1/-)	*Banding wheelbarrow wheel (6d.)*
New hatchet (2/8)	
Mend grate stand (1/-)	*Frost nails (4d.)*
New boiler stand	*Mend oven (8d.)*
Bottom grate 7lbs. (1/5)	*Rope turner (3d.)*
Mend oven (1/-)	*Boiler grate (2d.)*
Banding 2 wheels (1/9)	*Mend scythes (3d.)*
Mend pulper machine (1/-)	*Gate spring (4d.)*

The importance of the blacksmith to the rural community is clearly reflected by the large numbers of smiths to be found in the Welsh countryside. The census of 1831, for example, shows that there were 275 blacksmiths working in Cardiganshire in that year. Similarly, in 1851 the census shows that there were 250 blacksmiths in Anglesey, 335 in Brecknockshire and 520 in Caernarfonshire.

General Work—Continued.		
	s.	d.
New Drill Plough Share ...	7	0
Sharpening Share 8d. Do. Coulter	0	6
Stapling Whippletrees 9d. to 1s. per staple, and over according to size, re-stapling 6d. to 9d.		
Three Horse Iron Whipple ...	16	0
Ducks Foot Harrow, ¾ in. to 1½ inch	16	0
per piece		
,, Light weight ...	14	0
Steeling Duck Foot, per tooth ..	0	8
Sharpening Duck Foot, per tooth ...	0	3½
Straight Tooth Harrow, per piece ...	9	0
Steeling do. per tooth ...	0	5
Sharpening do. per tooth ...	0	2½
Welding Mower Driving Rod in centre	3	0
Do. at end ...	3	6
Fixing Blades in Mower Knife ...	2	0
Welding Mower Knife ...	3	6
Fixing Iron underneath wheel Drag in addition to the value of Iron.	3	6
Skid do. ...	3	0
Repairing Spindles, per head ...	2	0
Gate Hinges ¼ in. 8d. to 10d. per lb. according to length.		
Gate Hinges ⅜ in. 7d to 9d. per lb.		
Ordinary Fire Grates 8d. to 10d. per lb.		
Door Hinges and Trough Irons 8d. to 10d.		

Extract from a blacksmith's price list, 1918, showing the variety of work undertaken.

The smithy at the Vulcan Arms, Cwmbelan, Powys, c. 1895. James Morris, the blacksmith at the anvil.

PLOUGH-MAKING

In the eyes of many, the highest expression of the blacksmith's art was plough-making, and it was on his expertise in this aspect of the craft that his skill was judged. The deceptive simplicity of the implement's appearance and design belied the skill and experience necessary for its construction. Some blacksmiths gained widespread fame for the quality of their ploughs.

Amongst the most famous of the Welsh blacksmith plough-makers were Zachariah Jones of Corwen, Clwyd, and David Jones, Y Lion, near Cardigan in Dyfed. Very often such smiths worked in close conjunction with local foundries who would cast mould-boards and ploughshares to the smith's own designs. Many of these blacksmiths were themselves noted ploughmen and it was a widely held view that a man who could not plough himself could not be expected to

11

produce a good plough. Great interest was taken in ploughing competitions and the maker of a match-winning plough was assured of great prestige. Many of the large-scale plough manufacturers such as Howards of Bedford and Ransomes of Ipswich brought their latest models to such matches to demonstrate them to the local farming population. Blacksmiths were quick to take advantage of any improvements they saw in this way and to adapt them to suit local conditions. John Jones of Tal-y-bont, Powys, for example, produced just such an adaptation of a Ransome's plough which was known locally as the 'three-quarter patent plough'. Robert Phillips, a blacksmith of Penpont, Brecknockshire, charged between £2. 7s. and £2. 10s. for his ploughs during the 1840s, and the last plough to be made at Aberbanc forge, during the first decade of this century, was sold for £9.

Thomas Thomas of Ffostrasol, Dyfed, holding the no. 8 plough which he manufactured. The photograph was taken in 1937.

Craftsmen on the village square at Ysbyty Ifan, Gwynedd, 1904. The three blacksmiths, Job Hughes (shoeing), Gruffydd (repairing the plough) and John Henry (banding) were brothers. Griffith Owen, the wheelwright, can be seen shaping a wheel-spoke. His workshop stood directly across the road from the smithy.

TYRING

The blacksmith often worked with other village craftsmen to produce various specialized items. He made wooden ploughs jointly with the carpenter and he was often called upon to help the woollen manufacturer with the making and repairing of machinery. The craftsman most closely linked to the blacksmith was the wheelwright, and the two often had their workshops located in close proximity. The blacksmith made all the elaborate metal fittings for the carts and wagons and was also responsible for banding the wooden wheels made by the wheelwrights. Banding or tyring — the fixing of metal tyres on to wooden wheels — was possibly the most spectacular of all the tasks performed at the smithy involving as it did a great deal of noise, steam and

Tyre bender in use at Rhydgaled Smithy, Nanhoron, Gwynedd, c. 1910.

clamour. To avoid distractions many blacksmiths devoted certain days exclusively to banding and on such days a number of wheels were completed.

It was vitally important to make the tyre the exact size required. Too large a tyre could easily work loose and cause an accident whilst too small a tyre could crush a wheel. A traveller, a small wheeled instrument with a short handle, was used to measure the circumference of the wheel. It was pushed around the rim of the wheel

and the number of revolutions it made were counted. To ensure absolute accuracy in this task many smiths insisted on repeating the operation three times before the iron was cut to the required length. Once cut, the iron was bent cold to shape using a tyre bender. The more primitive benders simply consisted of a post on to which a rounded block of wood was bolted with a metal 'stop' above it. The iron was pushed in between the block and the stop and pulled downwards until the desired curvature was achieved. By the late nineteenth century, however, this had been displaced by a tyre-bending machine which consisted of a series of three metal rollers mounted on a stand. Such machines were hand cranked and could be adjusted according to the required curvature. Finally, the ends of the tyre were joined together and fire-welded.

Before the tyre could be fitted on to the wheel, it first had to be heated so that it would expand slightly. Some smithies had hearths which were large enough to allow the work to be undertaken indoors, but in most cases this task had to be performed outside on a makeshift fire. Once the bands were sufficiently heated they were carried from the fire by two men using long-handled tongs or purpose-made tyre dogs and dropped over the wheel which had been clamped onto a metal tyring platform. The tyre was then rapidly hammered into position and doused with water to prevent the wheel catching fire. Banding was always a spectacular operation involving a great deal of frenetic activity, and in many parts of Wales the difficulty of the task was recognized by a gift of *cwrw bando* (tyring beer) to the smith. The price charged for tyring varied enormously according to the size of wheels and the amount of metal needed for the tyre. John Williams, of Cellan in Dyfed, charged 6*s.* a pair for banding cart wheels, in the 1850s. Half a century later, blacksmiths in the same county charged anything from 17*s.* to 21*s.* per set depending upon the width of the band.

Top: *Preparing a wheel for banding.*
Bottom: *Heating the tyre.*

Overleaf
Top: *Carrying the tyre to the platform.*
Bottom: *Cooling the heated band.*

OTHER SKILLS

Whilst the world of the rural blacksmith was one of routine tasks, many of them did gain a reputation for their skill in a particular branch of the craft. Plough-makers have already been mentioned in this context, others gained renown for making harrows, tempering iron, making edge tools etc. David Davies, Felin-fach, near Tre-lech a'r Betws in Dyfed established a widespread reputation as a maker of reaping hooks. The smithy was equipped with a water-wheel which was used to drive the sharpening stone and the lathe on which the tool handles were turned. Interestingly, the country blacksmiths never managed to produce a satisfactory scythe blade and these were imported from English foundries, although they were often set by the local blacksmith. Andrew Davies of Ciliau Aeron, and later Aberaeron, in Dyfed, similarly established himself as a maker of reaping hooks. At the turn of the century, his son David began manufacturing the characteristic long-handled Aberaeron shovel. When the works closed in the 1940s, 'Morthwyl Mawr Aberaeron', the large tilt hammer which he used was removed and can now be seen at the Welsh Industrial and Maritime Museum in Cardiff. The Aberaeron shovel continued to be made in Cardiganshire by Griff Jenkins, a blacksmith in Cwrtnewydd.

A few blacksmiths became so proficient in certain aspects of the craft that there was a call for their services from other smiths. One such was Jack Millet, 'Pincher Jack' a blacksmith from Crickhowell, Powys, who travelled the countryside making pincers for other smiths. Itinerant nail-makers also travelled the countryside at one time making large batches of shoeing nails for the local smiths. Some blacksmiths ventured outside the traditional spheres of activity of the craft. Arthur Williams of Llandybïe, Dyfed, for example, whose father Moses was a noted maker of agricultural implements, established himself as a well-known manufacturer of bicycles. In 1880 he began making a 'penny farthing' and five years later introduced a safety bicycle. Similarly, John Williams (Ioan Madog), the noted blacksmith-poet from Porthmadog devised the *pedfuanydd*, a lever-operated velocipede, in 1856. Later, in 1870, he patented an 'expanding jumper' rock drill and

'Morthwyl Mawr Aberaeron', the Aberaeron tilt hammer, now at the Welsh Industrial and Maritime Museum, Cardiff.

in 1873 invented a self-acting sand-box for the Ffestiniog Railway. A few ventured into even more unlikely fields. John Williams of Llanddeusant achieved a certain reputation, if not notoriety, as a blacksmith-dentist as did his namesake in the nearby village of Llansawel, whilst John Owen of Moelfre in Clwyd was also the local barber.

FARRIERY

Most blacksmiths spent a large part of their time shoeing the vast numbers of horses which were needed on the land. Although farriery and blacksmithing were technically distinct crafts, the majority of rural smiths combined both and obtained a significant proportion of their income from shoeing. Indeed, most estimates suggest that the majority of smiths spent at least half of their time with horses. In one week in January 1900, for example, Ben Evans of Aberbanc shod fifteen horses, for which he charged 2s. 4d. for a set of new shoes and 1s. for re-nailing old ones. By the end of the First World War, not only had prices increased significantly, but farriery had been formalized to a certain extent. The Newcastle Emlyn and District branch of the Master Farriers' and Smiths' Union, of which Evans was secretary, had established a standard set of charges for all shoeing work as the illustration on page 19 demonstrates. As recently as the Second World War, a certain Edward Parry, a blacksmith in the Anglesey market town of Llangefni, recalled shoeing 500 horses in one year, eleven of them on the same day.

In more recent times the majority of blacksmiths used machine-made horseshoes and nails, although at one time, virtually up to the beginning of the twentieth century, every smith had to make his own. Making horseshoes required great skill. The shoe was fashioned out of a piece of iron the length of which was determined by the width of the horse's foot (the ratio between the two measurements varied between $2\frac{1}{2}$ times to $3\frac{1}{7}$ times the width of the foot according to which smith one spoke to). The iron was heated, centred, and bent into a V shape before being rounded into a horseshoe. Finally the calkin (the turned down heel of the shoe), clips and nail holes were fashioned. Any slack time in the smithy was usually spent building up stocks of shoes for regular customers.

Horses were brought into the smithy to be shod and were usually held by the handler or tied to a ring in the wall. Some smiths used a tripod-like farrier's stand to rest the hoof for shoeing. Most, however, decried this as being somehow below their professional dignity and preferred to hold the hoof between their legs whilst the work was done. Usually, the front feet were seen to first to allay the horse's nervousness. Once the old shoe was removed the foot was prepared for the new one. The hoof was cleaned with a small knife known as a *searcher,* and the point of the buffer; trimmed with a paring knife and finally smoothed with a rasp. The new shoe was tried for size and any necessary adjustments made. It was then black-heated and placed on the hoof to seat it. Despite the clouds of smoke and acrid burning smell at this stage, the horse suffered no distress as the burning material was not living tissue. Great care had to be taken in nailing the shoe to avoid damaging the sensitive flesh of the foot. Once the nails appeared at the front of the hoof their points were clenched to hold the shoe firmly in position. Blacksmiths used a light, whippy handled claw-hammer for shoeing, and a long pointed metal rod known as a *pritchel* to hold the hot shoe in position. All the farriery tools were kept in a wooden box and were never removed for any other purpose.

A horse's hoof grows continually and has to be trimmed regularly. In the case of farm-horses working on soft land it was often necessary to do this before the shoes themselves became worn out. In such cases the old shoe was removed, the hoof was pared and trimmed and the old shoe replaced. This was normally charged for at a rate slightly over half the sum paid for shoeing with new shoes. At the time when iron was a particularly expensive commodity it was customary to keep worn-out shoes to be used in the making of new shoes. This iron was held to be the property of the farmer concerned and worn shoes were stored in a wooden box branded with the owner's initials. It was customary in many areas to provide the blacksmith with an allowance of beer (usually half a gallon) for shoeing a young horse. Interestingly, in some parts of Montgomeryshire he forefeited this right should he fail to clinch the first nail. By the beginning of this century, the allowance of beer had largely been commuted to cash and, as is illustrated opposite in the Newcastle Emlyn Farriers price list, the extra payment for shoeing young horses stood at 3s. in 1919. The same price list shows that a similar premium of 5s. 6d. was charged for shoeing restless horses. In some areas these young horses were felled and bound or put in specially constructed stocks for shoeing.

In the days before veterinary surgeons became commonplace in the countryside, blacksmiths frequently acted as horse doctors, and as such were vital figures in a horse-based economy. Even after the advent of the vet some farmers continued to bring their horses to the smith to be treated for minor ailments. Indeed, up to the First World War, and beyond, in some

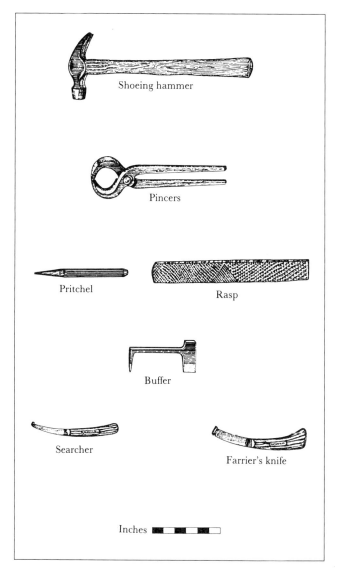

The farrier's tools.

districts, horses suffering from lampas, a painful swelling on the inside of the mouth, were brought to the smith to have their gums seared with a red-hot iron.

Price list — shoeing.

THE BLACKSMITH IN THE COMMUNITY

In many districts, the blacksmith's shop became an important social centre where people assembled to talk and gossip during their leisure hours. This was especially the case in Nonconformist Wales where the strong temperance tradition precluded the use of the village pub in this capacity. The smithy was always open, because the smith usually worked very long hours, all the work brought to him being claimed to be 'urgent'. During the winter months the smithy also had the advantage of being dry and warm. Farmers were said to visit the smithy on the slightest pretext and their

visits often lasted the entire evening as they swapped stories and exchanged gossip with the others who happened to be there. When large numbers of youths chanced to be in the smithy at the same time, the place became the scene of contests of strength, horseplay and mischief. Many blacksmiths saved simple repetitive tasks for these 'social' hours so that they too could enjoy and participate in the general banter and still carry on with their work. At Aberbanc smithy in Dyfed, for example, nailing boots and clog-irons were tasks reserved for Saturday afternoons, another occasion when the smithy was usually full of people.

The majority of regular customers had accounts with the blacksmith which they settled at regular intervals, mostly of six months or a year. Even then it was not unusual for there to be a long delay before the bill was actually paid and most blacksmiths complained of having a lot of their money 'out', i.e. owing to them from customers. It was also quite common for the blacksmith to receive part or all of his payment in kind,

David Griffiths, Defynnog, Powys, making a hoop, c. 1939.

and butter, corn, meat, eggs, wool and a host of other agricultural products were given to him. In parts of south-west Wales, a small stack of corn known as *llafur golym* (literally sharpening corn) was given to the blacksmith for all the small sharpening and tempering work undertaken on the implements of cultivation during the course of the year. These were all small tasks individually, but taken over the year amounted to a considerable sum. The practice appears to have died out shortly before the First World War, the last load of *llafur golym* being delivered to the smithy at Felin-fach, Dyfed, in 1912.

Some farmers also defrayed part of the cost of their blacksmith's bill by carrying coal and iron for the smith. At one time this could involve long journeys to the coal-mines, but more recently to the nearest railway station.

Usually the smithy's supply of coal was delivered annually and this could involve anything up to a dozen teams. Consequently it was a big day for both parties. The horses were bedecked in all their finery with their best harness, glistening brasses and colourful ribbons as farmers vied with each other in the appearance of their teams. It was an equally important occasion for the blacksmith who was responsible for providing food and drink for the helpers. Copious amounts of drink were a traditional part of these festivities and this was often continued despite the restrictions imposed by temperance. In some areas too the blacksmith reciprocated by assisting his regular customers with the harvest, all of which helped to bind the community closer together.

Llawr-y-glyn Smithy — the Building

The smithy originally stood at the centre of the small village of Llawr-y-glyn in the western part of the former county of Montgomeryshire, now Powys. Basically an eighteenth-century building, it was much modified during the nineteenth century. It ceased to operate as a smithy in 1963 and the building was offered to the Welsh Folk Museum in 1969 by the then owner, Mr Tom Bennett, Y Felin, Llawr-y-glyn. Dismantling work began in September 1970 and the smithy was re-erected at St Fagans during 1971–72. It was opened to the public in 1973.

The smithy is a simple single-storey structure with a lofted stable at the northern end. The building (12.2m long and 4.9m in width) is made up largely of local stone in a random rubble construction with wide mortar joints. Many of the stones appear smooth and rounded which suggests that they might have been obtained from the brook which ran behind the building at its original site. Some of the walls are partially weatherboarded with ¾ inch oak planks fixed onto a wooden frame, a characteristic feature of the vernacular architecture of this part of Wales. The building has a gabled roof of small local slates with a tiled ridge. The slates are held by iron pegs. There is a rectangular stone chimney at the central gable with a second, smaller brick chimney at the gable end of the projecting hearth. A series of stepped dripstones project from the central gable protecting the junction with the roof of the lower section of the building. At present there is cast-iron guttering along the entire front of the building although the original arrangement was far more rudimentary with home-made guttering above the two doors and the front window only. The building has three wooden-framed windows, two with small glazed panes and one unglazed. Both the unglazed windows in the gable end and the large windows to the front have planked shutters. Finally, the smithy has two doorways, both at the front. There is a pair of large double half-doors, with a removable central pillar, to the shoeing area at the right of the building; a second pair of half-doors to the stable on the left, with a further half-door above to allow entry to the loft.

The building has a simple three-unit plan, although there is some evidence to suggest that the present layout may be the culmination of a whole series of modifications over the years. There is certainly physical evidence in the form of the internal woodwork and a change in the pitch of the roof to suggest that the central portion of the building was extended forward at one stage. Similarly, linguistic evidence could be taken to imply that the pentice, the shoeing area at the southern end of the building, is a later addition: the word 'pentice' itself being the dialect term in that part of Montgomeryshire for an extension to a building, as well as being the word for a shoeing area in a smithy. The blacksmith's house, also known as *Yr Efail* (The Smithy) stood to the south of the smithy at an angle to it.

The pentice (4.4m × 3.1m) is entered through a pair of large double doors at the front. There is a small unglazed window in the wall on the right of the room. The floor is pitched with small rounded stones although the room originally had a beaten earth and shale floor. On the wall opposite the door there is an iron ring which was used to tether horses whilst they were shod. A planked wooden partition separates the pentice from the smithy itself. A square opening in this partition was used to pass horseshoes from the smithy to the shoeing area. It is interesting to note that the partition is covered with a series of branded initials, the result of testing branding-irons and pitchmarks made at the smithy. Spare horseshoes and lengths of banding iron were also stored on hooks along the wall. This room contained only the essentials of the farriers craft, the shoeing box, a farrier's stand and a shovel and a broom for keeping the floor clean.

The central room, the smithy itself, is entered through a doorway in the partition; it measures 7m × 4.7m and also has a pitched floor. There is a large window (1.3m × 1m) in the front wall and a smaller window (1m × 0.7m) on the right-hand wall of the projecting hearth. The smithy has two hearths. The largest hearth (2.3m ×

1.2m) stands opposite the door and has a metal cowling to draw off the smoke. This was the main hearth where the blacksmith himself worked and was large enough for the heaviest work, including the heating of tyres. A second, smaller hearth (1.7m × 1m) stands at the gable end of the room and has a canopy of wattle and daub. This was originally used by the apprentice and also for shoeing. Both hearths now have hand-operated long bellows; although the smaller hearth had circular bellows during the latter days of its use. For reasons of visitor circulation and safety, the smaller hearth is the one used for demonstration purposes at the Museum.

Each hearth has its own anvil. Alongside each anvil is a water trough which was used for quenching the hot metal. A stone trough is used in conjunction with the working hearth, and a metal one with the main hearth. The smithy is fitted with two work benches, the largest one near the front window and a smaller one along the partition. Each bench is fitted with a leg or staple vice which has a long metal bar running into the floor. This absorbs the shock of any blows and allows the vice to be used for heavy work. Each bench also has a smaller vice for lighter work. To the right of the small hearth is a block-mounted drilling machine. Alongside the

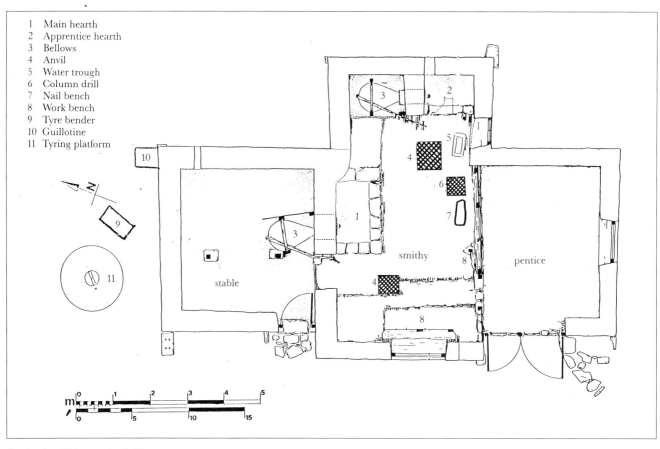

1 Main hearth
2 Apprentice hearth
3 Bellows
4 Anvil
5 Water trough
6 Column drill
7 Nail bench
8 Work bench
9 Tyre bender
10 Guillotine
11 Tyring platform

Interior plan of Llawr-y-glyn Smithy.

Llawr-y-glyn Smithy during dismantling work, 1970. The blacksmith's house can be seen on the right.

partition is a nineteenth-century bench from St Nicholas near Cardiff used for making horseshoe nails. It is wooden, supported on a post and two stick legs and has a small iron anvil for pointing the nails. Most of the hand tools in the smithy belonged to Mr T.J. Thomas, a blacksmith at Maesteg, Mid Glamorgan. A few tools, most notably the bick-irons (small T-shaped anvils) were at one time used at Llawr-y-glyn.

Beyond the smithy is the stable, a small square room (3.7m × 3.7m) which was originally used to house horses awaiting shoeing, but was little used in recent years. It has the framework for a half-loft intended for the storage of iron, but more recently employed as a drying rack for scythe handles, for which the smithy was well-known locally. The stable now has a beaten earth floor although there is evidence to suggest that it did at

23

one time have a pitched floor. The large wooden cupboard against the gable wall is of modern construction.

There are several features worthy of note outside the building. To the right of the pentice door is a shallow, stone-lined pit used to collect horse droppings brushed out from the shoeing area. Another area delineated in stone is to be found behind the pentice where the coal was stored. A hand-turned grindstone is also to be found there. On the other side of the projecting hearth was a corrugated iron lean-to shed built against the stable wall and used to store iron. Immediately to the north of the smithy is the tyring area. Its most obvious feature is the tyring platform itself which consists of a circular metal plate 1.7m in diameter mounted on a low stone base. The platform is from the village smithy at St Fagans (now demolished) and was moved to the Museum in 1970. There was no tyring platform at Llawr-y-glyn, the banding being undertaken on a makeshift platform erected at the front of the smithy itself. At the corner of the building is a lever operated guillotine-type metal cutter and a tyre-bending machine. This machine stands on a wooden framework and was made towards the end of the nineteenth century by T. Jones and Sons, Priory Foundry, Carmarthen, well-known manufacturers of agricultural implements. According to local tradition there was also a ramshackle pigsty built against the front wall of the stable, but no evidence of this remains.

John Rowlands, the blacksmith at Llawr-y-glyn at the turn of the century. A portable tyring platform can be seen leaning against the smithy wall.

A portable tyring platform of the type used at Llawr-y-glyn. This example comes from Penybont Fawr, Clwyd.

Llawr-y-glyn in the 1860s

A vivid picture of the life and work of the Llawr-y-glyn smithy during its heyday in the second half of the nineteenth century emerges from an account book now preserved in the archive of the Welsh Folk Museum. The book which covers a period of five years during the late 1860s was kept by the blacksmith, Andrew Humphreys, and was generously donated to the Museum by one of his successors, D.P. Morgan, Llawr-y-glyn's last blacksmith. The first entry in the book is dated 6 April 1865 and it continues until 12 May 1870. For those five years Humphreys' meticulously kept accounts provide us with an illuminating glimpse of the economic and social significance of the blacksmith during the period.

Llawr-y-glyn village is situated in the upper reaches of the narrow Trannon valley, which cuts into the upland mass of west Montgomeryshire. The district once served by the smithy is mountainous with the land rising from 600 feet on the valley floor to over 1,400 feet in the moorlands to the west. It is an area of high rainfall and poor soils, much of it now forested and a large part of it now lying under the waters of the huge Clywedog reservoir. During the nineteenth century, however, even these inhospitable moorlands supported a thriving agricultural community which depended upon the blacksmith for its iron-working requirements. The farming was predominantly pastoral with an emphasis on sheep rearing although there was a significant arable component on the lower land. The area was sparsely populated and the smithy served farms hidden amongst the many steep-sided valleys and scattered over the surrounding open moorlands. The account book lists forty regular customers, all but two of whom were farmers. The exceptions were a corn mill and a fulling mill, both of which were situated near the village itself. The farms ranged in size from twenty-five acres to 1,249

acres and averaged almost 300 acres, but it must be remembered that the larger farms tended to be mountain holdings with vast tracts of poor moorland. Many of these mountain farmers faced a long and difficult journey over hilly and rugged terrain to the smithy.

Judging from the account book, Andrew Humphreys was typical of the hundreds of rural blacksmiths to be found throughout Wales in that the variety of his work was enormous. For example, an extract for May 1868 from the account of Nicholas Bennett, Glan-yr-afon, one of the largest customers, demonstrates the blacksmith's versatility:

7 May	Mending a umbrella		0.9
8	2 new shoes 2 removed		1.4
Do	1 ring hook		0.2
11	4 shoes removed piecing heels		1.4
Do	new suck (plough share) 1 plate 21½lbs		9.0
Do	fettling plates 3 nuts 3 pins		1.0
Do	coltiron (coulter) repaired		0.6
13	1 new shoe 3 removed		1.0
16	2 new shoes ? 2 removed		1.2
18	1 shoe removed		0.2
21	Mending a drill	[?]	½.0
Do	1 staple sharping forke		0.3
25	4 shoes removed		0.8
27	fettling a plough 1 ciplin (coupling)		1.0
28	1 new shoe 1 removed		0.8
Do	Iron to plough		1.6
Do	1 pin 14 nails		0.6

Several things emerge from this extract which shed some light on the blacksmith's work. Firstly, the frequency with which customers visited the smithy, and the large number of separate tasks which the blacksmith undertook for his customers in one month. It is interesting to note also the prevalence of farriery in the blacksmith's work.

Llawr-y-glyn smithy was said to have a good reputation for shoeing horses and this is confirmed by the accounts which show that Humphreys spent half his time working with horses. In January 1866, for example, Humphreys listed 173 completed tasks in the book and no fewer than fifty-two per cent of these were horse-related. During the month he put on thirty-three sets of

Group standing in the pentice door (i.e. the entrance to the shoeing area) at Llawr-y-glyn.

new shoes at a cost of 2*s.* per set, removed thirty-six shoes at a cost of 2*d.* each and performed twenty-one other farriery tasks. An analysis of individual farm accounts similarly reveals that between forty and fifty per cent of the work done was farriery based.

The account book also testifies to the variety of goods produced by Andrew Humphreys and the range of skills he was called upon to use. He produced a variety of agricultural utensils from simple items like nails (6 for 1*d.*), staples (1*d.*), pig rings (1½*d.*), through hand tools like dung hooks (1*s.* 3*d.*), pikles (2*s.*), hay hooks (1*s.*), mattocks (1*s.* 8*d.*) and spades (3*s.* 9*d.*) to large complex implements like ploughs (£3. 1*s.* to £3. 5*s.*), harrows (£2. 7*s.*), chain harrows (£2. 3*s.* 6*d.*) and rollers (£1. 13*s.* 8*d.*). The importance of sheep in local farming is reflected by the numerous references to pitchmarks (1*s.*) and shears in the account book. Humphreys also produced several kinds of edge tools including billhooks (2*s.*), cleavers (2*s.* 6*d.*), hay knives (2*s.* 6*d*) and axes, which varied in price according to weight (e.g. a 1lb axe cost 3*s.* 4*d.*). A lot of

D.P. Morgan, Llawr-y-glyn's last blacksmith, shoeing.

the smithy's products were made for local craftsmen, especially the wheelwright, and there are frequent references to 'cart fittings' 'iron to waggons', strakes, strake nails and bands all of which were charged for according to weight of iron used. The blacksmith also made gates, hinges, hammers and a host of other items. Finally, he also turned out a range of domestic fittings and household utensils such as candlesticks (1*s*. 6*d*.),

candlepans (2*s*. 9*d*.), curtain rods and hooks (4*d*.), pots (8*d*.) and door knockers (2*s*. 6*d*.).

The accounts also shed some interesting sidelights upon less obvious aspects of the district's economy. Humphreys made several peat irons (2*s*. 6*d*.) for instance, peat being the main fuel used on the upland farms. He also made several peeling irons or barking irons — small blunt instruments used for stripping bark

D.P. Morgan and his family standing in the pentice door.

from trees. Oak bark in particular was rich in tannin and was highly prized for tanning. The spring bark harvest was an important element in the rural economy in which large numbers of people took part. Another, less respectable, source of income for some was poaching and the account book shows that Humphreys also produced 'drivers', illegal barbed fishing spears, when the occasion demanded.

Not all Humphreys' time was spent in making things, however, and the book testifies to the fact that he spent a fair proportion of his time repairing and maintaining iron goods for the community. Again most of his work was undertaken for the farming community. Keeping the implements of cultivation in good working order provided the blacksmith with a great deal of work and during the busy spring months the books contain almost daily references to the sharpening of harrow tines (1*d.* each), the tempering of shares and coulters, and the

Repairing a mowing machine at Llawr-y-glyn during the 1950s.

mending of various parts of ploughs, harrows, drills and cultivators. It is clear from the account book that at Llawr-y-glyn these small routine tasks were charged for individually and not allowed to accumulate over the year as in south-west Wales. Other items repaired included various pieces of harness, shovels and rakes. He also helped local craftsmen with the tempering and sharpening of edge tools such as chisels (½*d.*), saws (8*d.*) and hammers (6*d.*). Finally, he also repaired a variety of domestic utensils including lanterns (3*d.*), stoves (2*d.*), coffee pots (2*d.*), box irons (3*d.*) and butter churns (1*s.*

3*d.*). Humphreys seems never to have been deterred by the complexity of the item and there are references to his turning his hand to the repairing of locks, clocks and guns.

Humphreys would appear to have sent out his bills annually, as most payments were made in late spring and early summer. The majority of farmers cleared their accounts annually, although a few customers did pay by instalments. In November 1865, for instance, a certain William Jones, Esgeiriaeth, paid £2 towards his bill of £4. 17*s.* 5*d.* and cleared the balance on 20 February

1866. Similarly, Maurice Jones, Ty'n-yr-wtre, paid off £3 of his £5. 18s. 11½d. bill on 27 November 1865 and cleared the balance the following month. The vast majority of payments were made in cash although a few farmers paid a proportion of their bills in kind. In April 1866, for example, Edward Edwards, Waen-y-gittin, virtually cleared his account of £1. 4s. 4½d. with a sheep and a goose valued at 15s. and 9s. respectively. Andrew Jones, Gwernafon, paid part of his £7. 0s. 5½d. bill with a bag of oats valued at 18s. and a bag of wheat worth £1. As might have been expected, David Lloyd, the local miller, similarly paid the greater part of his £2. 13s. 9d. bill with two bags of wheat worth £2. Several of the upland farmers supplied Humphreys' domestic heating needs with peat which was valued at 3s. per load.

They also indirectly helped him to meet his smithing fuel needs by transporting coal from the railway station to the smithy. Many of them indeed defrayed part of their bills in this way. Thomas Jones, Tan-lan, for example, was allowed 8s. 7d. for carrying 1 ton 5 cwt.

3 qt. of coal from Llanidloes station on 15 August 1867. In 1869 the same farmer carried a further 17 cwt. of coal to the smithy. In January 1868 both Thomas Bennett Cil-haul, and Richard Jones, Neuadd-lwyd, were credited with bringing loads of coal to the smithy. For some reason Humphreys appears to have obtained iron from Caersws station rather than Llanidloes, which was marginally closer. In April 1867, Edward Edwards, Cwm-llimwynt, brought him 12 cwt. 3 qt. of iron and later in the same year Richard Owen, Ninfa, brought him a further 11 cwt. 1 qt. Humphreys further cemented his relationship with his customers by helping them with their harvest. On the 18 August 1869 he spent one day reaping for a certain Evan Evans and two days later he spent, '1 day at Harvest' for Andrew Jones, Gwernafon. In this, as in many other ways, the account book shows Andrew Humphreys to be typical of the hundreds of other blacksmiths working in the Welsh countryside during the second half of the nineteenth century.

The Blacksmith in the Twentieth Century

The blacksmith's position at the apex of rural craftsmanship began to be undermined as early as the final quarter of the nineteenth century. From that time onwards his story is one of slow decline with the smith gradually being relegated from his role as a truly creative craftsman to that of a service craftsman repairing and maintaining goods and implements made elsewhere. In this, the blacksmith's position resembles that of many other rural craftsmen who were unable to compete with the mass-produced goods which flooded into the countryside from the industrial areas. Before the First World War, for instance, ploughs manufactured by large English companies such as Ransomes, Howards and Hornsby had displaced the blacksmith-made ploughs from most of Wales. Even before that the blacksmith had ceased to be the sole manufacturer of edge tools. Large-scale manufacturers like Isaac Nash of Stourbridge, in the case of agricultural hand tools and William Marples of Sheffield in the case of general tools had long since cornered the market. Indeed, companies like Nash took over almost literally from blacksmiths in that they even continued to produce the traditional local patterns of hand tools for them. Nash's catalogue for 1899, for instance, contains ninety-four different local patterns of hooks and sickles, ninety billhooks, forty-six axes and hatchets and sixteen types of slashers. To add insult to injury many of these companies also produced blacksmith's tools often to a higher standard than those made by the blacksmiths themselves.

The blacksmith's livelihood, as opposed to his status as a creative craftsman, remained assured, however, as long as the horse continued to be the primary source of power on the land. The demand created by the vast numbers of horses needed on the farm ensured that the smith remained busy. Agricultural statistics show that the number of agricultural horses in England and Wales increased from 827,000 in 1870 to a peak of 981,000 in 1911. The resulting increase in farriery work must, to a certain extent, have offset the decline in the blacksmith's income from other sources. For this reason, therefore, the blacksmith retained his importance to the rural community for a while longer, albeit in a changed role.

The First World War, however, brought about a dramatic change even in that situation. The exceptional demands of wartime agriculture together with the needs of the military for horses ultimately led to the introduction of the internal combustion engine to agriculture. By 1920 twenty per cent fewer horses were employed on the land than had been the case only a decade earlier. Although this decline proceeded slowly throughout the inter-war years, well over half a million horses were still working on the farms of England and Wales at the outbreak of the Second World War. Once again exceptional wartime circumstances accelerated the process of change and by 1950 the number of farm horses had been halved. Although significant numbers of horses remained on the land throughout the fifties, by 1960 only 46,000 were left, a mere five per cent of the number less than half a century earlier. With the disappearance of the horse from the land, so too a whole

A former blacksmith's shop at Felin-fach, Powys, now a garage: the fate of so many rural smithies.

way of life crumbled. Amongst the main casualties of this change were the craftsmen who were almost entirely dependent upon the horse for their livelihood, most notably the wheelwright and the saddler. Blacksmiths by virtue of their diverse skills escaped extinction, but their numbers became severely depleted. The dramatic decline in the number of blacksmiths is exemplified by the case of the Newcastle Emlyn and District Farriers and Smiths Union. In 1918 the association boasted seventy members, but by the early 1960s, fewer than half-a-dozen of the smithies listed had survived.

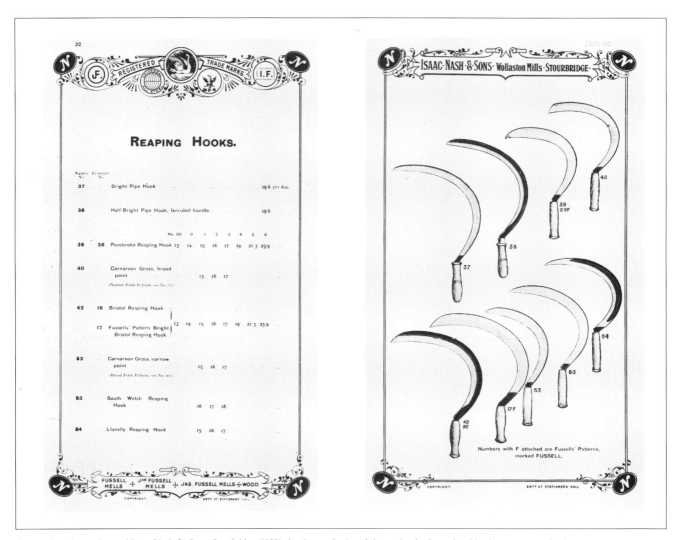

Extract from the catalogue of Isaac Nash & Sons, Stourbridge (1899) showing a selection of the reaping hooks produced by the company at the time.

Shoeing at Defynnog, Powys, shortly before the Second World War.

Many smiths simply gave up the unequal battle and left their craft for more lucrative employment. Older craftsmen struggled on in the face of reduced incomes until they retired and were never replaced. Even where a business remained viable, however, it often proved difficult to attract youngsters into the craft because of what they viewed as its uncertain future. It is significant, in this context, that many of the businesses which did survive were family concerns where the son followed the father into the craft. Large numbers of blacksmiths diversified their interests, concentrating on the viable aspects of their craft until they eventually ceased to be blacksmiths at all. It was often a natural step for the smith to break from traditional blacksmithing into allied fields like agricultural engineering, metal fabrication and motor repair. Many of the largest garages, agricultural implement dealers and contractors in rural Wales have evolved over a couple of generations from a humble blacksmith's shop.

Unlike the case of many of the other rural craftsmen, however, the demand for the blacksmith's traditional skills never completely disappeared, as the number of smiths still working today testifies. After a period of rapid contraction when the number of blacksmiths fell dramatically, the number of rural blacksmiths would now appear to be in equilibrium with the demand for their services. Today's blacksmith draws his customers from a much wider area, or indeed quite often travels from farm to farm to carry out his work. He has diversified his products to take advantage of the increased demand for wrought ironwork and even the tourist industry. Electric power has replaced much of the heavy hand work; he has oxy-acetylene and a host of modern equipment to assist him but he still retains many of the basic skills of his predecessors. Whilst it is unlikely that the rural blacksmith will ever again recapture the same prominent position in the community which he enjoyed in his heyday, his future does at least seem to be assured. There is every reason to think that many of the blacksmiths' shops in rural Wales will continue to echo to the ringing sound of hammer upon anvil and the air will still be filled with the characteristic smell of horses being shod for the forseeable future.

Acknowledgements

The publication of this booklet was only made possible by the kind help and co-operation of many people. My first duty is to thank those numerous Welsh blacksmiths who gave so freely of their time and knowledge and whose tape-recorded reminiscences, preserved in the Welsh Folk Museum sound archive, form the basis of this book. I am also indebted to my colleagues: Dr Elfyn Scourfield for the use of his field notes taken during the removal of the smithy from Llawr-y-glyn to St Fagans; Mr Gerallt D. Nash for the plans of the building; Mr Arwyn Lloyd Hughes for his archival expertise; Mr Kevin Thomas for the photographs and Ms Christine Stevens for reading the manuscript. I would also like to thank Mr David Rees Edwards, the Museum's blacksmith, for his expert advice on technical aspects of the craft and his patience in performing the role of photographic model. Finally, I am particularly indebted to Ms Elizabeth Forrest of the Museum Schools Service for her splendid line drawings.

Further Reading

J. Bailey, *The Village Blacksmith* (Princes Risborough, 1977)

COSIRA, *The Blacksmith's Craft* (London, 1963)

I. Edwards, *Davies Brothers, Gatesmiths* (Cardiff, 1977)

W.K.V. Gale, *Ironworking* (Princes Risborough, 1981)

J. Starkie Gardner, *Ironwork* I & II (London, 1927 & 1930)

I. Niall, *Country Blacksmith* (London, 1966)

F.W. Robins, *The Smith* (London, 1953)

R. Webber, *The Village Blacksmith* (Newton Abbot, 1971)